Sandwiches

Recipe	page	calories/portions	classic	sophisticated	filling	portable	fast	eat now	make ahead	easy
Spicy Roast Beef Sandwich	6	370		●		●				●
Ham Sandwich with Arugula	7	380		●	●					
Club Sandwich	8	650	●			●				
Italian Panini	10	460				●	●			●
Marinated Chicken Breast Sandwich	10	720		●	●				●	
Bacon, Lettuce, & Tomato Sandwich	12	400	●			●				
Smoked Chicken Sandwich	13	620		●	●					●
Steak & Avocado Sandwich	14	820		●	●			●		
Bacon & Egg Sandwich	14	810			●			●		●
Paté Sandwich	16	310		●			●			●
Smoked Pork Sandwich with Sauerkraut	17	720	●					●		
Turkey Orange Sandwich	18	710		●	●			●		
Ham & Brie Sandwich	18	230			●	●	●			●
Smoked Salmon Sandwich	22	370		●			●			●
Tuna, Caper, & Olive Sandwich	23	420				●	●			●
Pan Bagnat	24	720		●	●			●		
Sardine Sandwich	26	510					●	●		●
Smoked Whitefish Sandwich	26	240				●	●			
Crabmeat Sandwich	27	380		●		●				
Egg Salad Niçoise Sandwich	28	680		●					●	●
Shrimp "Poor Boy"	28	650	●	●				●		
Garlicky Eggplant Sandwich	32	800				●			●	
Blue Cheese & Walnut Sandwich	32	450		●						●
Smoked Tofu Sandwich	34	570				●	●			●
Santa Fe Cheese Sandwich	35	550		●				●	●	
Creamy Avocado Sandwich	36	350		●					●	●

Recipe

Recipe	page	calories/portions	classic	sophisticated	filling	portable	fast	eat now	make ahead	easy
Fruit & Goat Cheese Sandwich	36	340		●			●		●	◐
Greek Salad Sandwich	38	710			◐				●	
Falafel Sandwich	38	710		●	◐				●	
Chanterelle Salad Sandwich	40	630		●					●	
Green Egg Sandwich	41	600		●						◐
Sandwich Provençal	42	520		●	◐			◐		◐
Sun-Dried Tomato-Avocado Sandwich	42	360			◐		●	◐		
Hamburger	46	660	◐		◐			◐		◐
Bacon-Cheeseburger	47	770	◐		◐			◐		◐
Green Burger	48	630		●	◐			◐		
Italian Burger	48	640		●	◐			◐		
Blue Burger	50	600		●	◐			◐		
Curried Turkey Burger	51	560		●	◐				●	
Fish Burger	52	480		●			●	◐		
Tofu Burger	52	400		●					●	
Onion Rings	54	280	◐					◐		
Baked Potato Chips	54	110	◐					◐		
Spiced Popcorn	55	130	◐						●	
Veggie Slaw	55	100		●					●	
French Toast Sandwich	58	440	◐					◐	●	◐
Raspberry Delights	59	350		●			●			◐
Banana Nut Sandwich	59	530	◐	●			●			◐
Cherry-Walnut Sandwich	60	230		●			●			◐
Watercress Tea Sandwich	60	110					●		●	◐
Iced Choco-Mint Sandwich	61	120		●			●		●	◐
Cucumber-Mint Tea Sandwich	61	120		●			●		●	◐

Table

The History of the Sandwich

John Motagu, 4th Earl of Sandwich, invented the "meal between the slices" that has retained his name. The Earl lived in England during the 18th century. He was a passionate card player, and did not want to leave the card table even to eat a meal. The Earl asked his attendant to bring some bread and topping right to the table—and he no longer had to interrupt his game. From England, the sandwich came to the USA, where the biggest sandwich culture developed a foothold. This is not surprising, as many Americans enjoy easy and uncomplicated food—especially food that is fast and easily transportable.

American lifestyles seem to get busier and busier, so sandwiches fit in nicely. Most sandwiches are easy to prepare. Of course, this does not mean that sandwiches cannot be enjoyed leisurely—perhaps even with a glass of wine, to add a touch of sophistication.

The Bread

Good ingredients are important for a good sandwich, and this starts with, of course, good bread. Fortunately, today there is a rich assortment of delicious, artisanal breads in bakeries, specialty stores, and supermarkets.

Many sandwich recipes call for sandwich bread, or whole-grain bread. These, of course, are readily available in any supermarket.

Baguettes often differ greatly in size and weight; for that reason you will find their weight noted in the recipes.

Meat & More

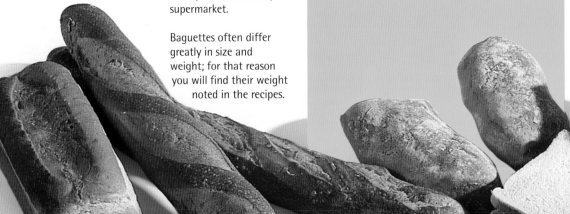

The same is true for ciabatta (Tuscan country bread) and focaccia (Italian flatbread).

Depending on personal preference, you can vary the type of bread used in a recipe. However, the size and consistency of the substituted bread should not be too different from the one suggested, in order to have good texture and balance in the sandwich.

A Few Sandwich Guidelines

• If you use good quality, fresh ingredients, your sandwich is guaranteed to be tasty!
• Thick bread, such as some baguettes and French rolls, can be scooped out a bit in the middle, to prevent the sandwich from being too bulky.
• Lettuce, herbs, and other leafy greens should be washed and well dried before using in a sandwich.
• Use a sharp knife to cut through the sandwich; a serrated bread knife is ideal.
• When cutting the sandwich, hold it with your fingertips, making a "tunnel" underneath. Insert the knife between your thumb and fingers, underneath your hand, to make the cut (see photo on page 8).
• Cut very carefully, without much pressure, using a back-and-forth motion. Square sandwiches look pretty when cut diagonally.
• Using clear plastic wrap, wrap the sandwich tightly for storage or transport, so that nothing falls or drips out.
• Always serve a sandwich with a napkin, or take one along in your lunch bag or picnic basket.
• Accept that something always falls out when eating a sandwich. Then, enjoy nibbling on the escaped ingredients.
• Allow yourself and your friends or family to delight in licking one's fingers after eating the sandwich—it's part of the fun!

Many of the items needed to make a good sandwich are already on hand in the refrigerator or pantry, for example, butter, mayonnaise, mustard, lettuce, eggs, cheese, and sliced meats and poultry. Other good sandwich ingredients include fresh herbs, tomatoes, cucumbers, and even fruit. Pick up some fresh bread, and you can create your own spur-of-the-moment sandwiches from what you have in the house.

From left to right: White loaf, baguettes, Italian rolls, sandwich bread (large and small) dark rye bread, sesame rolls, French rolls, focaccia

Spicy Roast Beef Sandwich

● portable
● easy

Serves 2:

2 tbs mayonnaise
2 tbs sour cream
2 tbs spicy mustard
Salt & pepper to taste
1–2 tsp prepared
  horseradish
1/2 bunch fresh watercress
2 large poppy-seed rolls
4 oz roast beef, thinly
  sliced
1 clove garlic

Prep time: 20 minutes
Per portion: 370 calories
14 g protein / 28 g fat / 17 g
carbohydrates

1 Mix together the mayonnaise, sour cream, and 1 tsp of the mustard. Season with salt and pepper. Stir in the horseradish to taste.

2 Trim and wash the watercress. Split the rolls in half. Spread all of the roll halves generously with the horseradish-mayonnaise mixture.

3 Divide the watercress among the bottom roll halves. Top the watercress with the roast beef slices.

4 Peel and mince the garlic. Spread the roast beef with the garlic and the remaining mustard. Top the sandwiches with the top roll halves.

Ham Sandwich with Arugula

● sophisticated
○ filling

Serves 2:

1 red bell pepper
6 oz oyster mushrooms
2 tbs butter
Salt & pepper to taste
1/2 bunch arugula (about 2 oz)
6 slices white sandwich bread
2 1/2 oz Black Forest ham, sliced

Prep time: 30 minutes
Per portion: 380 calories
23 g protein / 10 g fat / 53 g carbohydrates

1 Preheat the grill or broiler. Trim and wash the red pepper and cut it lengthwise into eighths. Grill or broil the pepper pieces for about 8 minutes (if broiling, place the peppers on a foil-lined pan skin-side up), until the skin blackens and blisters. Let the peppers cool under a kitchen towel, then remove the skin (see step 5, page 24).

2 Meanwhile, clean the oyster mushrooms, and cut them into pieces if very large.

3 Melt 1 tbs of the butter in a skillet over medium-high heat. Add the mushrooms and sauté for 5 to 7 minutes, until golden brown. Season with salt and pepper. Add the red pepper pieces and sauté for 2 minutes.

4 Wash the arugula and pat dry. Toast the bread, let it cool slightly, then spread all slices with the remaining 1 tbs butter.

5 On 3 slices of the bread, layer the arugula, mushrooms, ham, and red pepper, dividing evenly. Top with the remaining slices of bread and slice each sandwich once diagonally.

Club Sandwich

● portable
● a classic

Some sources claim that the famous club sandwich was invented more than a hundred years ago at the Saratoga Club in New York State. Others state that the club sandwich was first served in the elegant club cars of the streamliner trains. These trains were—as was the club sandwich originally—double-deckers.

Serves 2:

2 eggs (optional)
2 tbs butter
6 oz boneless turkey breast
Salt & pepper to taste
4 slices bacon
1 large ripe tomato
2-3 lettuce leaves
3-4 dill pickles (optional)
2 slices whole-grain
  sandwich bread
4 slices white sandwich
  bread
2 tsp grainy mustard
2 tbs mayonnaise

Prep time: 35 minutes
Per portion: 650 calories
34 g protein / 34 g fat / 66 g
carbohydrates

1 Boil the eggs (if using) for about 10 minutes, until the yolks are hard-cooked. Soak them briefly in ice water, peel and cool.

2 In a skillet, heat 1 tbs of the butter over medium heat. Add the turkey and sauté for about 5 minutes on each side, until cooked through. Transfer the turkey to a plate, season with salt and pepper, and cool. Add the bacon to the skillet and cook until crisp; drain the bacon on paper towels.

3 Wash the tomato, remove the stem, cut into thin slices, and season with salt and pepper. Wash the lettuce leaves and pat dry. Slice the eggs crosswise. Slice the pickles lengthwise (if using). Cut the turkey into thin slices.

4 Toast the bread and let it cool slightly. Spread the whole-grain bread on both sides with the remaining butter. Spread the mustard over 2 slices of the white bread, and mayonnaise over the other 2 slices.

5 Layer the ingredients in this order, making 2 sandwiches: the mustard-

spread bread, lettuce, turkey, tomatoes, whole-grain bread, ham, eggs, (if using) pickles, (if using) and on top with the mayonnaise-spread bread.

6 Press the sandwiches together lightly. Carefully slice them diagonally with a sharp knife. To secure the sandwich halves, insert a frilly cocktail toothpick through the layers from top to bottom.

Variations
The club sandwich is made slightly differently in different areas. Some times ham is used instead of bacon, or chicken is used instead of turkey. Choose your own favorite meats.

Tip! Skewering the sandwiches prevents the layers from falling apart. Don't use a simple toothpick, which is hard to see, and could cause an injury while eating. Look for special sandwich picks, which have colorful fringes at one end. In addition to holding the sandwiches together, these festive picks make sandwiches look pretty.

Italian Panini

● fast
● portable

Serves 2:

15–20 leaves arugula
2 oz Parmesan cheese
4 slices Italian bread
2 tsp pesto
2 tbs crème fraîche
2 oz prosciutto (or other
favorite Italian meat),
thinly sliced

Prep time: 10 minutes
Per portion: 460 calories
27 g protein / 22 g fat / 39 g
carbohydrates

1 Wash the arugula and pat it dry. Finely grate the Parmesan cheese.

2 Spread 2 slices of the bread with the pesto, and the other 2 slices with the crème fraîche.

3 On the pesto-spread pieces of bread, layer the arugula, prosciutto, and Parmesan. Top with the remaining pieces of bread. Cut the sandwiches in half and serve.

Marinated Chicken Sandwich

● prepare ahead
● sophisticated

Serves 2:

About 8 oz boneless
chicken breasts
1 fresh red chile
1/4 cup olive oil
3 tbs lemon juice
1 tbs chopped fresh sage
1 small zucchini
1 small clove garlic
Salt to taste
A few leaves frisée lettuce
or curly endive
2 French rolls, or 1/2
baguette (about 8 oz)
2–3 tbs mayonnaise

Prep time: 30 minutes
Marinating time: 3 hours
minimum, better overnight
Per portion: 720 calories
29 g protein / 42 g fat / 59 g
carbohydrates

1 With a small sharp knife, score the chicken breasts in a few places. Wash the chile, cut it in half lengthwise, and remove the seeds. Set aside one chile half for another use; chop the other half finely. In a shallow bowl, mix the chopped chile with 3 tbs of the olive oil, 2 tbs of the lemon juice, and the sage. Add the chicken, toss to coat well with the marinade, cover, and chill for at least 3 hours, or ideally overnight.

2 Wash and trim the zucchini. With a vegetable peeler, cut the zucchini lengthwise into thin slices. Peel and mince the garlic, and place it in a shallow bowl. Stir in the remaining 1 tbs each of olive oil and lemon juice, and season with salt. Add the zucchini slices, toss to coat well with the marinade, cover, and chill for about 3 hours.

3 Preheat the broiler. Wash the lettuce and pat it dry. Place the chicken breast on a large piece of aluminum foil on a baking sheet. Broil the chicken for about 7 minutes on each side, until it is golden brown and cooked through. Cut the chicken into 1/2-inch-thick slices, and season with salt.

4 Split open the rolls or baguette. If using the baguette, cut it in half crosswise. Spread the bottom bread pieces with the mayonnaise. Arrange the chicken breast pieces on top, and drizzle with the pan juices, if desired.

5 Top the chicken with the marinated zucchini. Cover with the top bread pieces and serve.

Tip! You can also sauté or grill the chicken breast: In a skillet, heat 2 tbs butter over medium heat. Add the chicken breast and sauté for 8-10 minutes, until golden brown on both sides and cooked through. Or, grill the chicken over a medium-hot charcoal fire for about 7 to 10 minutes per side.

above: Marinated Chicken Sandwich
below: Italian Panini

Bacon, Lettuce, & Tomato Sandwich

- a classic
- portable

Serves 2:

8 slices bacon
A few leaves romaine
   lettuce (or other crisp
   lettuce)
2 ripe tomatoes
4 slices sandwich bread
2 tbs mayonnaise
Salt & pepper to taste

Prep time: 20 minutes
Per portion: 400 calories
13 g protein / 25 g fat / 29 g
carbohydrates

1 Place the bacon in a nonstick skillet and fry over medium heat until crisp and brown. Drain the bacon on paper towels.

2 Wash the lettuce and pat it dry. Wash the tomatoes, remove the stems, and cut the tomatoes into thin slices.

3 Toast the bread and spread 1 side of each slice of bread generously with the mayonnaise.

4 Layer the lettuce and tomato on 2 of the bread slices, season with salt and pepper, then top with the bacon. Cover with the remaining bread slices.

5 Cut the sandwiches in half diagonally, and serve.

Variation

Bacon, Lettuce, and Avocado Sandwich: substitute 1/2 avocado mashed with a few drops of lemon juice for the tomato.

Smoked Chicken Sandwich

● sophisticated
● filling

This sandwich is deceivingly simple and super delicious. Rather than being eaten on the side, the coleslaw is put right between the slices of bread.

Serves 3:

Coleslaw:
1 red bell pepper
1/2 small head green cabbage (about 10 oz)
1/2 cup mayonnaise
2 tbs grainy mustard
Salt & pepper to taste

About 1 lb boneless smoked chicken breast (or sliced smoked turkey breast)
6 large slices rye bread

Prep time: 20 minutes
Marinating time: 1 hour
Per portion: 620 calories
36 g protein / 36 g fat / 38 g carbohydrates

1 For the coleslaw: Wash and trim the red pepper and cabbage, and cut or shred them thinly. In a medium bowl, mix together the mayonnaise, mustard, and salt and pepper. Add the red pepper and cabbage, mix well, and let the mixture stand, covered, for 1 hour to blend the flavors.

2 Remove the skin from the chicken breast. With your fingers, pull the chicken into small pieces, or cut it into long, narrow strips.

3 Place 3-4 tbs of the coleslaw on each of 3 slices of the bread. Arrange the chicken on top of the slaw. Cover with the remaining slices of bread. Cut the sandwiches in half, and serve the remaining coleslaw on the side.

Tip! Use this coleslaw as a side dish for other sandwiches. Look for a tasty variation of this classic recipe on page 55.

Steak & Avocado Sandwich

- filling
- sophisticated

Serves 2:

2 lemons
1 small onion
1 clove garlic
Salt & pepper to taste
About 10 oz cooked steak,
  thinly sliced
1 ripe avocado
4–6 leaves Belgian endive
  (or 2 large leaves
  romaine lettuce)
4 slices light rye bread
2–3 tbs Lemon Aïoli
  (p 21)
1 tbs canola oil

Prep time: 25 minutes
Marinating time: 1 hour
Per portion: 820 calories
40 g protein / 49 g fat / 50 g
carbohydrates

1 Squeeze the juice from the lemons. Peel and chop the onion and garlic, place them in a bowl with 1/4 cup of the lemon juice, and puree with a hand blender (or use a regular blender). Add 1/4 tsp each of salt and pepper. Spread the mixture on the steaks and let them marinate, covered, in the refrigerator for 1 hour.

2 Cut the avocado in half, remove the pit, peel, and cut into slices. Immediately drizzle the avocado with the remaining lemon juice.

3 Wash the endive thoroughly and pat dry.

4 Spread the bread slices with the Lemon Aïoli. Arrange the endive leaves on 2 slices of the bread.

5 In a large, heavy skillet, heat the oil over medium-high heat. Add the steaks, and reduce the heat slightly. Pan-fry the steaks for 1 1/2 minutes on each side to heat; they should still be a bit pink inside.

6 Thinly slice the steak across the grain. Arrange the steak on the endive leaves, top with the avocado slices, and season with salt and pepper. Cover with the remaining bread slices. Cut the sandwiches in half, and serve.

Tips! For a quick version of the aïoli, mix purchased mayonnaise with 1 clove garlic, minced. Stir in 1 tsp finely grated lemon zest. This sandwich can be a messy one, so it's best to serve it on a plate, with a knife and fork.

Bacon & Egg Sandwich

- eat now
- filling

Serves 2:

1 red bell pepper
2 green onions
6 oz mushrooms
2 tbs canola oil
Salt & pepper to taste
10 slices bacon
5 eggs
2 tbs chopped fresh herbs
  (such as parsley, dill,
  basil, and/or tarragon)
1/2 round focaccia (about
  6–7 oz)
Soft butter for spreading

Prep time: 30 minutes
Per portion: 810 calories
36 g protein / 42 g fat / 70 g
carbohydrates

1 Wash and trim the red pepper, and cut it into 3/4-inch squares. Trim and wash the green onions, and slice them into fine rings. Clean the mushrooms and cut them into fine slices.

2 In a skillet, heat the oil over medium heat. Add the pepper and sauté for about 5 minutes. Add the onions and mushrooms and sauté for another 5 minutes. Remove the skillet from the heat and season the vegetables with salt and pepper.

3 In a nonstick skillet, fry the bacon until crisp. Drain on paper towels.

4 In a bowl, beat the eggs, then stir in the herbs, salt, and pepper. Pour the egg mixture into the skillet with the bacon fat, cover, and cook over low heat for 3 minutes. Spread the vegetables on top of the eggs, then remove from the heat.

5 Cut the focaccia in half through the diameter. If it is very thick, pull some of the bread from the middle of the loaf. Spread butter over the bottom half of the bread. Place the eggs on top, and crumble the bacon over them. Cover with the top of the bread. Cut the sandwich in half or quarters, and serve.

top: Bacon & Sandwich
bottom: Steak &
Avocado Sandwich

Paté Sandwich

● fast
● sophisticated

Serves 2:

3 oz mushrooms
1 small clove garlic
1 tbs butter
Salt & pepper to taste
2 sprigs fresh marjoram or
    oregano
1 sprig fresh Italian
    parsley
2 large slices dark rye
    bread (or black or
    pumpernickel bread)
3 oz country-style paté (or
    liverwurst)

Prep time: 15 minutes
Per portion: 310 calories
11 g protein / 19 g fat / 25 g
carbohydrates

1 Clean the mushrooms
and cut them into slices.
Peel and mince the
garlic. Heat the butter in
a skillet over medium
heat, add the garlic, and
sauté it briefly. Add the
mushrooms, and sauté
for about 10 minutes,
until softened. Transfer
the mixture to a plate,
season with salt and
pepper, and cool.

2 Wash and shake dry the
herbs. Pick off the parsley
leaves and chop them;
pick off the fresh
marjoram leaves and
leave them whole.

3 Spread the bread slices
with the paté, dividing
evenly. Spread the
mushrooms over 1 slice.
Sprinkle the parsley and
marjoram over the
mushrooms and cover
with the remaining slice
of bread. Cut the
sandwich in half and
serve immediately.

Tip! You can also serve
the sandwiches open-
faced, a great option for
a party. Increase the
amount of mushrooms to
4 oz, and spread them on
both slices of bread. Cut
the sandwich into bite-
size pieces.

Smoked Pork Sandwich with Sauerkraut

● a classic
● eat now

Serves 2:

1 onion
2 tbs canola oil
2 tbs mayonnaise
1 tsp prepared horseradish
2 rye rolls
2 tsp mustard
4 oz smoked pork loin,
  thinly sliced
4 oz sauerkraut (drained)
2 slices Swiss cheese

Prep time: 20 minutes
Per portion: 720 calories
16 g protein / 64 g fat / 23 g
carbohydrates

1 Peel the onion and cut it into fine rings. Heat the oil in a skillet over medium heat, add the onion rings, and sauté until golden brown.

2 Mix together the mayonnaise and horseradish. Slice open the rolls. Spread the bottom halves of the rolls with the horseradish-mayonnaise, and spread the top halves of the rolls with mustard.

3 Preheat the broiler, or heat the oven to the highest temperature. On the bottom halves of the rolls, layer the pork loin, sauerkraut, onion rings, and cheese. Bake or broil the roll halves for 5 minutes, until the cheese is melted. Cover with the top halves of the rolls and serve warm.

Variation

Reuben Sandwich: Replace the pork loin with sliced corned beef or pastrami. You can also substitute Thousand Island dressing for the mustard.

Turkey-Orange Sandwich

● sophisticated
● filling

Serves 2:

1 orange
3-4 tbs mayonnaise
2 tsp grainy mustard
1 tbs sour cream (or crème fraîche)
Pinch of chili powder
Salt to taste
1 tbs butter
8 oz boneless turkey breast
2-4 leaves crisp lettuce
1 small avocado
1 tbs lemon juice
1/2 baguette (about 8 ounces)

Prep time: 30 minutes
Marinating time: 1 hour
Per portion: 710 calories
40g protein / 31 g fat / 69 g carbohydrates

1 Wash the orange with hot water, then dry it. Grate about 1 tbs of the orange zest, and mix it with the mayonnaise, mustard, sour cream, and chili powder. Season with salt and refrigerate for 1 hour to blend the flavors.

2 Cut the orange in half, squeeze the juice from 1 half, and cut the other half into slices. Cut off the peel from the orange slices, then cut the slices into quarters.

3 Heat the butter in a skillet over medium heat. Add the turkey breast and sauté for about 10 minutes, until cooked through. Remove the turkey from the pan and cut it lengthwise into thin slices. Stir the orange juice into the pan drippings and cook for 1 minute. Return the meat to the pan and turn it in the sauce several times.

4 Meanwhile, wash the lettuce and pat it dry. Peel the avocado, cut it in half, and remove the pit. Cut the avocado into slices, drizzle it with lemon juice, and season with salt.

5 Cut the baguette in half, and slice both halves open lengthwise. Spread 1 tbs of the orange-mayonnaise mixture on each of the halves. Layer the lettuce, turkey, avocado, and orange slices on the bread, and spread the remaining orange-mayonnaise mixture on top. It's best to eat this sandwich with a knife and fork.

Variation

Turkey-Cranberry Sandwich: Instead of the avocado, use 1/4 cup whole-berry cranberry sauce.

Ham & Brie Sandwich

● fast
● portable

Sometimes sweet and salty create a wonderful, sophisticated contrast. This sandwich is proof of it!

Serves 2:

1 tbs honey
1 tbs grainy mustard
2 tbs alfalfa sprouts
2 leaves crisp lettuce
2 onion rolls
2 1/2 ounces Brie cheese
2 slices cooked ham (about 2 oz)

Prep time: 10 minutes
Per portion: 230 calories
9 g protein / 11 g fat / 26 g carbohydrates

1 Stir together the honey and mustard. Wash the alfalfa sprouts and lettuce leaves and pat them dry. Cut the lettuce into strips.

2 Slice open the onion rolls, and, depending on their thickness, remove a little bit of bread from the inside of the upper halves. Spread each of the lower halves with 1 tbs of the honey-mustard. Cut the Brie cheese into slices and place them on top of the honey-mustard.

3 Arrange the ham on top of the Brie, and spread with the rest of the honey-mustard. Distribute the lettuce and alfalfa sprouts on top.

4 Cover with the top roll halves, press down lightly, and serve.

Variation

Ham & Gouda Sandwich: Substitute young Gouda cheese for the Brie.

left: Turkey Orange Sandwich
right: Ham and Brie Sandwich

Mayonnaise is a must for many sandwiches, especially those made with fish and seafood. Though you can buy mayonnaise at the store, it tastes so much better when homemade. And it's surprisingly easy to make!

How to Make Mayonnaise

Have no fear—mayonnaise is easy to prepare. All you need is a fresh egg yolk, mustard, vinegar, oil, and spices. However, the oil for the mayonnaise should not be too strongly flavored. For this reason, olive oil is less suited to making mayonnaise, unless you enjoy its unique flavor, and it complements the sandwich ingredients. Good, neutral-flavored oils for mayonnaise include canola, sunflower, safflower, and vegetable oils. If you want to give the mayonnaise a nutty flavor, mix a little hazelnut or walnut oil into the neutral-flavored oil. Different types of mustards will also lend interesting flavor to homemade mayonnaise.

Basic Mayonnaise

Makes 1/2-3/4 cup:
1 very fresh egg yolk
1 tsp mustard
1 tbs white wine vinegar
1/2 cup canola oil
Salt & pepper to taste

Put the egg yolk and vinegar in a small bowl. Mix with an electric mixer on medium speed until blended.

While mixing, add the oil—at first drop by drop, then as a thin stream—until a thick mayonnaise is created. Season with salt and pepper. The mayonnaise keeps, tightly closed, for 2-3 weeks in the refrigerator. It goes well not only with sandwiches, but also in

Fish-wiches

salad dressings, and with meat, fish, or baked potatoes.

Variations

Aïoli: Replace the vinegar with lemon juice, and add 1-3 minced cloves of garlic, to taste.

Lemon Aïoli: To regular Aïoli, add the grated zest of 1/2 lemon.

Mint Mayonnaise: Replace the vinegar with lemon juice, and stir into the completed mayonnaise 2 tbs finely chopped fresh mint leaves. Refrigerate for at least 1 hour to blend the flavors.

Tip! It you are concerned about the raw eggs in your area, you can use pasteurized frozen egg yolks (2 tbs equals 1 egg yolk).

Sandwich Party

Sandwiches can easily be prepared ahead of time—a boon for the busy host. For a casual get-together, make a selection of sandwiches and arrange them on the buffet. You can select them according to a specific theme. For example, an American-themed party might include Spicy Roast Beef Sandwiches, BLTs, Club Sandwiches, Steak and Avocado Sandwiches, and Shrimp Poor Boys.

For a nice presentation, make the sandwiches with sandwich bread, cut them diagonally, and garnish them with colorful cocktail toothpicks.

Or, try a make-it-yourself sandwich bar: Arrange a selection of breads, fillings, garnishes, and condiments on a buffet. Guests can make their own sandwiches according to their tastes. Not only is this a very practical way for busy hosts to entertain, it fosters conversation among the guests.

Buffet Suggestions
• A variety of breads and rolls, prepared ahead of time: Baguettes should be cut into serving portions, sliced open, and have excess bulkiness removed. Pita bread and rolls should be split open in advance. If offering regular sandwich bread, place a toaster near it on the buffet
• Several kinds of sliced cheeses, cream cheese, and crumbled sheep's milk, goat's milk, and/or blue cheese
• Ham, salami, and paté
• Sliced roast beef or steak
• Sliced smoked or unsmoked turkey and/or chicken breast
• Tuna, cooked shrimp, and/or smoked salmon
• A variety of lettuce leaves or other salad greens, washed and spun dry
• Sliced tomatoes, cucumbers, onions, and pickles
• Chopped fresh herbs
• Sliced avocado, mango, or pear (remember to drizzle these with lemon juice to discourage discoloration)
• Butter, sour cream, or crème fraîche

• A variety of condiments, such as mayonnaise, mustard, ketchup, and ready-made sauces such as pesto
• Peanut butter, jam, honey
• Salt and pepper
• Side dishes, such as coleslaw, potato chips, and/or salads
• Silverware and napkins

Smoked Salmon Sandwich

● fast
● sophisticated

This sandwich combines a number of traditional "New York-style" ingredients. For a breakfast (or anytime) treat, substitute bagels for the rye rolls.

Serves 2:

1-2 green onions
1/4 cup radish sprouts (or watercress)
4 oz cream cheese, softened
1 tbs sour cream
1 tbs lemon juice
1 tbs chopped fresh dill
2 large rye rolls
4 oz thinly sliced smoked salmon (lox)
Pepper to taste

Prep time: 15 minutes
Per portion: 370 calories
19 g protein / 23 g fat / 24 g carbohydrates

1 Trim and wash the green onions, and slice them into fine rings. Wash the radish sprouts and pat them dry.

2 Stir together the cream cheese, sour cream, lemon juice, green onions, and fresh dill to make a creamy paste.

3 Slice open the rolls, and spread half of the cream cheese mixture on the bottom roll halves. Double-fold the salmon slices, place them on top of the cream cheese, and sprinkle with pepper.

4 Top each sandwich with 2 tbs of the radish sprouts. Cover with the top roll halves and serve.

Tuna, Caper, and Olive Sandwich

● fast
● portable

Serves 2:

1 can water-packed white
    tuna (6 oz)
1 tbs capers (drained)
10 black olives (pitted)
2 tbs Lemon Aïoli (p 21)
1 tbs sour cream (or crème
    fraîche)
Salt & coarsely ground
    pepper to taste
2 leaves crisp lettuce
1/2 baguette (about 8
    ounces)

Prep time: 15 minutes
Per portion: 420 calories
29 g protein / 8 g fat / 55 g
carbohydrates

Variations

Classic Tuna Fish Sandwich: Omit the capers and olives and add 1 stalk of finely chopped celery.

Tuna-Pesto Sandwich: Mix the tuna with 2 tbs pesto, 1 tbs mayonnaise, and 2 tsp lemon juice. Season the mixture with pepper, and serve it on the baguette with lettuce and tomato slices.

1 Drain the tuna thoroughly, then break it into pieces with a fork or your fingers. Finely chop the capers and olives.

2 In a bowl, mix together the tuna, aïoli, sour cream, capers, and olives. Season with salt and pepper.

3 Wash the lettuce and pat dry. Split open the baguette, then cut it in half crosswise. Spread the lower halves of the baguette with the tuna mixture and top with the lettuce. Cover with the top halves of the baguette and serve.

Pan Bagnat

● make ahead
● sophisticated

Niçoise in origin, "pan bagnat" means "bathed bread," referring to the soft texture of this vinaigrette-soaked sandwich. You'll want to select a sturdy loaf of bread, which can stand up to the soaking.

Serves 2:

1 red bell pepper
1/3 cup extra-virgin olive oil
2 slices fresh tuna (about 8 oz)
Salt & pepper to taste
Lemon juice to taste
1 clove garlic
1 tsp Dijon-style mustard
2 tbs red wine vinegar
1-2 tomatoes (about 4 oz)
4 sprigs fresh basil
1/2 red onion
3-4 leaves romaine lettuce
2 French rolls
10 black olives (pitted)

Prep time: 40 minutes
Marinating time: 1-2 hours
Per portion: 720 calories
32 g protein / 46 g fat / 48 g carbohydrates

1 Preheat the grill or broiler. Trim and wash the red pepper, and cut it lengthwise into eighths. Grill or broil the pepper pieces for about 8 minutes (if broiling, place the peppers on a foil-lined pan skin-side up), until the skin blackens and blisters. Let the peppers cool under a kitchen towel.

2 Brush 1 tsp of the olive oil over a piece of aluminum foil. Place the tuna slices on it and grill or broil for 4 minutes on each side. Season with salt and pepper, drizzle with a little lemon juice, and cool.

3 Make the vinaigrette: Peel and mince the garlic and add it to a bowl. Add the mustard, vinegar, 1/2 tsp salt, pepper to taste, and the remaining olive oil. Mix the vinaigrette with a wire whisk until well blended.

4 Remove the stems from the tomatoes, and cut them into thin slices. Wash the basil, shake dry, and pull off the leaves. Peel the onion and slice it into thin rings. Wash the lettuce, pat dry, and chop it into small pieces. Break the tuna into pieces.

5 Remove the skin from the red pepper strips: Lift up the skin with a sharp knife, and then pull off the skin, starting from the tip.

6 Slice open the French rolls, remove some bulk from the inside, and drizzle each half with 1 tsp of the vinaigrette.

7 On the bottom halves of the bread, layer the ingredients in the following order, dividing evenly: the tomato slices, basil leaves, tuna, red pepper, and onion rings.

8 Toss the remaining vinaigrette with the lettuce and olives, and arrange on top of the onion rings. Cover with the top halves of the baguettes, and press together gently. Wrap the rolls in foil, and refrigerate for 1-2 hours before serving.

> **Tip!** The tuna is especially tasty if you grill it over charcoal. For a fast, but still tasty, version of this sandwich, substitute fresh strips of red pepper for the roasted pepper, and use high-quality tuna from a can (drain before using).

Sardine Sandwich

● fast
● make ahead

Serves 2:

1 red onion
1 stalk celery
1 tbs chopped fresh dill
1 tsp sour cream
1 tsp white wine vinegar
Salt & pepper to taste
2 French rolls
1 can sardines (3.75 oz),
  packed in mustard or
  water (drained)

Prep time: 10 minutes
Per portion: 510 calories
40 g protein / 20 g fat / 39 g
carbohydrates

1 Peel the onion and wash the celery. Dice both finely, and mix with the dill, sour cream, and vinegar. Season with a touch of salt (be careful—the sardines are very salty) and pepper.

2 Slice the rolls in half lengthwise, but leave them connected on one side. Remove some bulk from the tops and the bottoms of the rolls.

3 Divide the sardines among the rolls. Distribute the onion-celery mixture on top of the fish.

**above: Sardine Sandwich
below: Whitefish Sandwich**

Whitefish Sandwich

● fast
● portable

Serves 2:

2 hard-boiled eggs (see
  p 28, step 1)
1 cucumber
1 sprig fresh dill
4 slices sandwich bread
1 tsp Dijon-style mustard
1 tsp mayonnaise
4 oz smoked whitefish
Pepper to taste

Prep time: 15 minutes
Per portion: 240 calories
18 g protein / 8 g fat / 24 g
carbohydrates

1 Peel the eggs and cucumber and slice them both finely.

2 Wash the dill, shake it dry, and chop. Cut the crust off the bread.

3 Spread 2 slices of the bread lightly with mustard. Spread the remaining 2 slices with mayonnaise. Arrange the eggs, whitefish, dill, and cucumber on the mustard-spread bread, dividing evenly, and season with pepper. Cover with the mayo-spread bread, and press together gently. Cut the sandwiches in half diagonally and serve.

Crabmeat Sandwich

● sophisticated
● portable

Serves 2:

6 oz crabmeat
**4 oz artichoke hearts
   (from a can or jar)**
1 stalk celery
1 tbs sour cream
2 tbs Lemon Aïoli (p 21)
**1 tbs chopped fresh Italian
   parsley**
Salt & pepper to taste
**A few leaves iceberg
   lettuce**
2 French rolls

Prep time: 20 minutes
Per portion: 380 calories
18 g protein / 15 g fat / 45 g
carbohydrates

1 Drain the crabmeat
and artichoke hearts well.
With a fork or your
fingers, break the
crabmeat into pieces. Cut
the artichoke hearts into
quarters. Trim and wash
the celery, then chop the
celery finely.

2 In a medium bowl, stir
together the sour cream
and aïoli. Add the
crabmeat, artichoke
hearts, celery, and parsley,
mix well, and season with
salt and pepper. Wash the
lettuce and pat dry.

3 Slice the rolls in half
lengthwise, but leave
them connected on one
side. Press the rolls open

flat, then toast the rolls
until golden brown.

4 Place the lettuce on
the lower halves of the
rolls, then spread the
crabmeat mixture over
the lettuce, dividing
evenly. Fold over the top
halves, and serve.

> **Tip!** To preserve the
> delicate taste of the
> crabmeat, use water-
> packed artichoke hearts,
> rather than those that
> have been marinated
> with herbs or garlic.

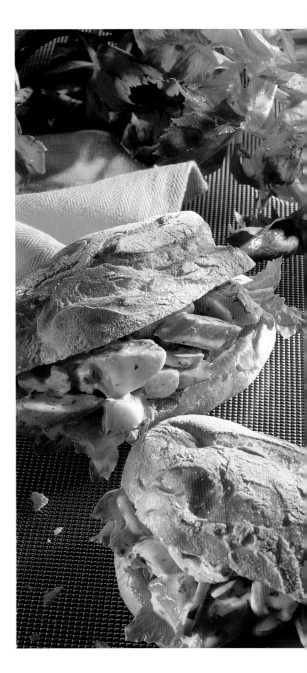

Egg Salad Niçoise Sandwich

● make ahead
● easy

Serves 2:
4 eggs
2-3 tbs mayonnaise
1 tbs chopped fresh chives
Salt & pepper to taste
3-4 anchovy fillets
2-3 oil-packed sun-dried tomatoes
2 large slices crusty white bread (or 4 small slices)

Prep time: 25 minutes
Per portion: 680 calories
30 g protein / 32 g fat / 78 g carbohydrates

1 Boil the eggs for 10 minutes, until the yolks are cooked hard. Plunge them into ice water for a few minutes. Peel the eggs, let cool slightly, then chop into large pieces, and place in a bowl. Stir in the mayonnaise and chives, and season with salt and pepper.

2 Rinse the anchovy fillets under cold water, and drain on paper towels. Cut the anchovy fillets and sun-dried tomatoes into long, thin strips.

3 Toast the bread slices until golden brown. Divide the egg salad among the slices of toast, spreading evenly. Cut the sandwiches in half, then top with the tomato and anchovy strips. Serve the sandwiches open-faced.

> **Tips!** Instead of whole anchovies you can use anchovy paste. Spread the paste sparingly on the bread slices, before adding the egg salad.
>
> To lighten this sandwich a little, replace the mayonnaise with sour cream, which has been mixed with 1/2 tsp Dijon-style mustard.

Shrimp Poor Boy

● sophisticated
● eat now

"Poor boys" are hero-style sandwiches originating in New Orleans. Be sure to serve this shrimp-based one with lots of napkins!

Serves 2:
8 oz shrimp
1/2 tsp salt
Pinch of cayenne pepper
Pinch of black pepper
3 green onions
3 tbs butter
2 tbs dry vermouth
1/4 cup lemon juice
2 tbs Worcestershire sauce
A few leaves of green leaf lettuce
1/2 baguette (about 8 oz)
1 tbs chopped fresh Italian parsley

Prep time: 20 minutes
Per portion: 650 calories
38 g protein / 22 g fat / 70 g carbohydrates

1 Peel the shrimp. With a small sharp knife, cut open the backs of the shrimp and remove the dark vein that runs down the length of them. Rinse the shrimp well and shake dry. Place the shrimp in a bowl with the salt, cayenne, and black pepper, and mix well.

2 Trim and wash the green onions, then slice them.

3 Heat the butter in a skillet over medium heat. Add the vermouth, lemon juice, Worcestershire sauce, and green onions, and simmer for 3 minutes. Add the shrimp, cover the pan, and simmer the shrimp in the sauce for 8-10 minutes, until they just turn opaque (take care not to overcook the shrimp or they will turn rubbery).

4 Meanwhile, wash the lettuce, pat it dry, and cut it into thin strips. Cut the baguette in half crosswise, then split open the halves. Remove a little of the bulk from all halves, then toast the halves until golden brown. Line the bottom of the baguettes with the lettuce, then top with the shrimp and sauce. Sprinkle the sandwiches with the parsley, and serve them warm.

above: Egg Salad Niçoise Sandwich
below: Shrimp Poor Boy

Almost every sandwich has it, and gains a crunchy, fresh quality because of it: the lettuce leaf! The selection is large. Besides the ubiquitous green leaf lettuce, there are many other kinds of lettuce that can be used to make sandwiches. For example frisee (light green curly lettuce), romaine (think Caesar salad), oak-leaf, and iceberg lettuces. Red-leafed radicchio has a fine, bitter nuance, but does not suit everyone's taste. Arugula is pleasantly pungent, and tastes slightly mustardy. Watercress has a very peppery and slightly pungent flavor.

Herbs and Sprouts

Fresh herbs are a wonderful, modern addition to many sandwiches. Try Italian parsley, dill, chives, and basil—all popular and versatile sandwich fillers. Fresh thyme, marjoram, sage, and tarragon lend unique flavor to sandwiches. Fresh mint is not only well suited for enhancing Asian-inspired sandwich fillings, but also for little tea sandwiches. For something even more exotic, try fresh cilantro.

Veggie Sand-wiches

Sandwich Veggies

Many kinds of sprouts, for example alfalfa, lentil, or radish sprouts, go well with sandwiches. Alfalfa sprouts are very neutral, whereas radish sprouts have a peppery flavor—these go well with smoked fish, roast beef, and ham.

Ready-Made Pastes and Sauces

Instead of mayonnaise or mustard, you can use ready-made pastes and sauces as highly flavorful sandwich spreads. Following are some good examples.
• Pesto is an Italian paste made from basil, Parmesan, oil, garlic, and finely ground pine nuts. Pestos made with other fresh herbs are starting to pop up on the market.
• Olive paste (also called tapenade) is made primarily from black or green olives, capers, and olive oil.
• Chutneys are sweet-sour mixtures made from fruits and vegetables, herbs, and spices. They go especially well with meat and poultry sandwiches.
• Nut and seed pastes are available in some

supermarkets, and natural and health foods stores. Besides the familiar peanut butter, you'll find almond, hazelnut, and cashew butters, which are well suited to tea sandwiches. Sesame paste (tahini), mixed with garlic and yogurt, goes very well with sandwiches made from broiled meat, vegetables and cheese—and, of course, garbanzo bean fritters (falafel).
• Chili sauces, mild or spicy, go well with meat and poultry sandwiches, but also with cheese-based sandwiches.
• Experiment according to your mood and taste with curry sauces, remoulade, guacamole, or another favorite type of sauce or dip.

About Calories

Most people like to pile sandwiches with a multitude of ingredients, which can make sandwiches rather high in calories. For those of us worried about cutting fat and calories, following are some suggestions to keep your sandwiches on the light side:
• Instead of using high-fat and -cholesterol regular mayonnaise, perk up light mayonnaise with lemon juice or other lively flavorings. Or, use mustard instead of mayonnaise, which is low in calories and contains no fat.
• Choose light versions of high-fat ingredients, such as yogurt, sour cream, and cream cheese. If you are layering lots of ingredients in your sandwich, you're less likely to miss the flavor from the high-fat ingredients.
• Experiment with reduced-fat cheeses. Many that are manufactured today have acceptable flavor and texture—especially when using them in a multi-ingredient sandwich.
• Choose low-fat, high-flavored meats and poultry, such as smoked turkey, marinated chicken, or water-packed tuna.

• Use a nonstick skillet for sautéing sandwich ingredients or burger patties, to reduce fat when cooking.

Sandwich Portions

Sandwiches come in many different sizes. Many of the recipes in this book serve 2 people generously. If a sandwich is cut into smaller pieces and served as hors d'oeuvre or snack, these recipes will serve up to double the number of people specified.

Clockwise from the top: Pesto, nut butter, guacamole, olive paste, aïoli

Garlicky Eggplant Sandwich

● portable
● make ahead

Serves 2:

1 eggplant (about 8 oz)
Salt
1 small clove garlic
1/4 cup olive oil
4–5 oz fresh mozzarella cheese (drained)
1/2 bunch fresh basil
1/2 baguette (about 8 oz)
Pepper to taste

Prep time: 45 minutes
Per portion: 400 calories
14 g protein / 25 g fat / 32 g carbohydrates

1 Wash and trim the eggplant, and cut it lengthwise into 1/4-inch-thick slices. Sprinkle both sides of the slices with salt, and let stand for about 20 minutes.

2 Meanwhile, peel and mince the garlic, and mix it with the olive oil. Thinly slice the mozzarella. Wash and shake dry the basil, then pull off the leaves. If the basil leaves are large, cut them into smaller pieces.

3 Preheat the broiler. Pat the eggplant slices dry with a paper towel, and place them on a foil-lined baking sheet. Brush the garlic oil thinly on both sides of the eggplant.

Broil the eggplant for 4 minutes on each side, until golden brown. Remove the eggplant from the broiler and brush one side again with the garlic oil.

4 Split open the baguette. Arrange 2 layers of eggplant slices on the bottom of the baguette, top with the mozzarella, and season with salt and pepper.

4 Distribute the basil leaves on the mozzarella. Drizzle the top part of the baguette with the remaining garlic oil, and place it on top of the basil. Cut the sandwich in half and serve.

> **Tip!** These sandwiches taste especially good with buffalo mozzarella, which you can find in specialty foods stores. Since it is made from the milk of Italian water buffaloes, this cheese is more expensive than cow's milk mozzarella—but it's worth the price!

Blue Cheese & Walnut Sandwich

● sophisticated
● portable

Serves 2:

2 tbs walnut halves
2 1/2 oz Roquefort cheese (or other blue cheese)
1–2 tbs small-curd cottage cheese
4 medium slices walnut bread
1–2 tbs walnut oil
1 firm, ripe pear
2 lettuce leaves

Prep time: 20 minutes
Per portion: 450 calories
14 g protein / 29 g fat / 37 g carbohydrates

1 Chop the walnuts, and toast them lightly in a dry skillet until light brown and aromatic. Remove the nuts from the pan and set aside.

2 Place the Roquefort and cottage cheese in a bowl, and stir with a fork until creamy.

3 Toast the bread slices until golden brown, cool slightly, then drizzle the slices evenly with walnut oil.

4 Wash and quarter the pear, then remove the core. Cut the pear quarters into thin slices. Wash the lettuce leaves and pat them dry.

5 Spread the cheese mixture on 2 slices of the bread. Sprinkle the walnuts over the cheese, and place a lettuce leaf on top of each slice. Distribute the pears on top of the lettuce, cover with the remaining bread slices, and serve.

> **Tip!** You can lighten this sandwich by using equal amounts of blue cheese and cottage cheese, and omitting the walnut oil.

above: Garlicky Eggplant Sandwich
below: Blue Cheese-Walnut Sandwich

Smoked Tofu Sandwich

- ● fast
- ● portable

Serves 2:

4 oz smoked tofu
4 oz mozzarella cheese
1 tomato
10–15 leaves arugula
4 slices whole-grain
  sandwich bread
2 tsp pesto
2 tbs sour cream (or crème
  fraîche)
Salt & pepper to taste

Prep time: 15 minutes
Per portion: 570 calories
30 g protein / 31 g fat / 50 g
carbohydrates

1 Cut the tofu and mozzarella into fairly thin slices. Wash the tomato and remove the stem. Cut the tomato into thin slices like the cheese.

2 Wash the arugula, pat it dry, and remove the large stems. Toast the bread until golden brown, and cool.

3 Spread 2 slices of the bread with the pesto; spread the remaining 2 bread slices with the sour cream.

4 On the sour-cream spread slices, layer the arugula, tofu, mozzarella, and tomato, and season with salt and pepper. Top with the pesto-spread slices. Cut the sandwiches in half diagonally and serve immediately.

> **Tip!** Look for good-quality smoked tofu in health foods stores and natural foods stores.

Santa Fe Cheese Sandwich

● eat now
● sophisticated

Some like it hot—this sandwich is fiery!

Serves 2:

1 tbs spicy chili sauce
2 tbs sour cream (or crème fraîche)
1 tbs lemon juice
A few leaves green leaf lettuce
Leaves from 4–6 sprigs fresh cilantro
1/2 red onion
1 small avocado
4 slices whole-grain sandwich bread
Butter (optional)
4 oz Monterey Jack cheese, sliced

Prep time: 20 minutes
Per portion: 550 calories
21 g protein / 31 g fat / 52 g carbohydrates

1 In a bowl, mix the chili sauce with the sour cream and 1 tsp of the lemon juice.

2 Wash and pat dry the lettuce and cilantro. Peel the onion and slice it into very fine rings.

3 Cut the avocado in half lengthwise, and remove the pit. Peel the avocado halves, cut them into slices, and drizzle with the remaining 2 tsp lemon juice.

4 Toast the bread until golden brown. Spread 2 of the slices with butter (if desired), then layer the lettuce, cheese, and avocado on top.

5 Divide the chili sauce mixture, onion rings, and cilantro leaves on top of the avocado. Cover with the remaining bread slices, cut in half diagonally, and serve.

Tip! For a mysterious, smoky flavor, substitute chipotle chiles in adobo sauce for the chile sauce: Remove 1-2 chiles from the can or jar, and mince them with some of their tangy sauce. Look for chipotles (actually smoked jalapeños) in Latin markets, or a well-stocked supermarket.

Creamy Avocado Sandwich

● sophisticated
● easy

Serves 2:

1 small clove garlic
1/2 onion
2/3 cup plain yogurt
2 tbs mayonnaise
3 tbs lemon juice
1 tbs chopped fresh Italian
   parsley
Salt & pepper to taste
1 head romaine lettuce, or
   other crisp lettuce
1 avocado
2 French rolls

Prep time: 20 minutes
Per portion: 350 calories
11 g protein / 14 g fat / 46 g
carbohydrates

1 Make the yogurt sauce: Peel the garlic and onion. Chop the garlic and onion finely, and place them in a bowl. Add the yogurt, mayonnaise, 2 tbs of the lemon juice, and the parsley. Mix the sauce well, and season with salt and pepper.

2 Wash the lettuce and shake dry. Tear the lettuce into large pieces. Cut the avocado in half, remove the pit, peel, and cut the flesh into dice. Drizzle the avocado with the remaining 1 tbs lemon juice.

3 Cut a slit into the sides of the rolls. With your fingers, remove most of the soft bread inside to create a pocket.

4 Spread the inside of each roll with 1 tbs of the yogurt sauce. Stuff the lettuce and avocado inside the rolls. Pour the remaining yogurt sauce over the lettuce, letting the yogurt sauce seep inside, and serve.

Variation

Fresh Tomato Sandwich: Substitute 1 perfectly ripe tomato for the avocado, and use herb vinaigrette instead of yogurt sauce. For the vinaigrette: Whisk together 1 tbs white wine vinegar and 2 tbs each walnut oil and olive oil. Stir in 1 minced clove of garlic and 1 tbs mixed chopped fresh herbs. Season the vinaigrette to taste with salt and pepper.

Fruit & Goat Cheese Sandwich

● fast
● sophisticated

Lightly tangy goat cheese and fruity, sweet mango make a fabulous combination. Try this sandwich as an unusual, but nutritious, breakfast.

Serves 2:

4 oz fresh goat cheese
2 tbs small-curd cottage
   cheese
1 ripe mango
2 sesame rolls

Prep time: 10 minutes
Per portion: 340 calories
16 g protein / 18 g fat / 28 g
carbohydrates

1 With a fork, mix together the goat cheese and cottage cheese until a smooth mixture forms.

2 Cut the mango flesh away from the pit. Peel the flesh, then cut it into slices.

3 Split open the rolls, toast them until golden brown, and cool. Spread the cheese mixture on the bottom part of the rolls, and top with the mango slices. Cover with the top parts of the rolls, and serve.

Variation

Substitute 2 peaches or 4 apricots for the mango.

> **Tip!** For a sandwich that is not quite so thick, divide the cheese and fruit among all 4 halves of the rolls, and serve them open-faced.

above: Creamy Avocado
Sandwich
below: Fruit & Goat Cheese
Sandwich

Greek Salad Sandwich

● prepare ahead
● filling

Eat this sandwich in summer, drink a Greek wine with it, close your eyes and imagine, you are sitting on a Greek island in a simple little tavern, its door painted blue.

Serves 2:

1 tomato
1 cucumber
1/2 red bell pepper
6 oz Greek sheep's milk cheese
1/2 red onion
15 Greek black olives (pitted)
2 tbs olive oil
1/2 tsp dried oregano
Salt & pepper to taste
2 small pita breads
2 tsp black olive paste (tapenade)

Prep time: 20 minutes
Cooling time: 1 hour
Per portion: 710 calories
22 g protein / 39 g fat / 70 g carbohydrates

1 Wash the tomato, quarter it, remove the stem, and chop the flesh. Peel the cucumber, cut it in half lengthwise, then cut it crosswise into 1/4-inch-thick slices. Wash and trim the red bell pepper, and chop it into small pieces.

2 Dice the cheese. Peel the onion and cut it into rings. Mix the above ingredients in a bowl with the olives, oil, and oregano. Season with salt and pepper and refrigerate for 1 hour to blend the flavors.

3 Toast the pita breads, then split them open to create a pocket. Spread the olive paste inside the breads. Stuff the salad into the pockets, dividing evenly, and serve.

> **Tip!** Olive paste can be found in well-stocked supermarkets, specialty foods stores, or natural foods stores.

Falafel Sandwich

● prepare ahead
● filling

Falafel are delicious little garbanzo bean fritters, a specialty of Middle Eastern cuisine.

Serves 4:
For the Falafel:
6 oz dried garbanzo beans
1 onion
2 cloves garlic
1/2 teaspoon salt
1/8 teaspoon pepper
1 tbs chopped fresh cilantro
1/2 tsp ground coriander
1 tsp ground cumin
Pinch of cayenne pepper
1/4 cup olive oil

Sesame Sauce:
1 clove garlic
1 2/3 cups plain yogurt
5 tbs sesame paste (tahini)
1 tbs lemon juice
Salt to taste

2 beefsteak tomatoes
Salt & pepper to taste
A few leaves of curly endive (or romaine lettuce)
4 small pita breads

Soaking time: overnight
Prep time: 50 minutes
Setting time: at least 30 minutes
Per portion: 710 calories
24 g protein / 29 g fat / 93 g carbohydrates

1 Soak the garbanzo beans overnight in water to cover by 2 inches.

2 The next day, drain the garbanzo beans well. Peel and chop the onion and garlic. Mix the onion and garlic with the garbanzos in a food processor and process until a paste forms. Mix in the salt, pepper, cilantro, coriander, cumin, and cayenne. Let the mixture stand for at least 30 minutes.

3 Form the garbanzo mixture into 8 small, flattened balls. In a skillet, heat the oil over medium heat. Add the falafel balls and fry for about 4 minutes on each side, until golden brown. Drain the falafel balls on paper towels and keep warm in a low oven.

4 For the sesame sauce: peel the garlic and mince. Mix it with the yogurt, sesame paste, and lemon juice. Season with salt.

5 Wash the tomatoes, remove the stems, and slice. Season the tomatoes with salt and pepper. Wash the endive, shake it dry, and cut it into thin strips.

6 Toast the pita breads, then split them open to form a pocket. Stuff each pita bread with endive strips, 2 falafel balls, and a few tomato slices. Drizzle each sandwich with 3-4 tbs of the sesame sauce, and serve.

Tip! Instead of soaked, dried garbanzos, you can use beans from a can. You'll need about 10 oz of drained canned beans for the recipe (about 2/3 of a 15-oz can). The leftovers can be used in a salad.

above: Greek Salad Sandwich
below: Falafel Sandwich

Chanterelle Sandwich

● prepare ahead
● sophisticated

Chanterelles—golden, trumpet-shaped exotic mushrooms—are prized for their woodsy flavor and tender texture. They can be found in specialty foods stores and upscale supermarkets. Choose another type of mushroom if desired.

Serves 2:

4 oz fresh chanterelle mushrooms (or other exotic mushrooms)
1 tbs butter
6 oz sheep's milk cheese
1 small fresh red chile
1 small red onion
1 clove garlic
1 tbs pine nuts
1/4 cup toasted sesame oil
1 tbs balsamic vinegar
1 tbs lemon juice
1 tbs chopped fresh basil
A few leaves of green leaf lettuce
2 sesame rolls

Prep time: 30 minutes
Marinating time: 30 minutes
Per portion: 630 calories
23 g protein / 26 g fat / 84 g carbohydrates

1 Trim the chanterelles, then wipe them clean with a damp cloth. If large, cut the chanterelles into smaller pieces. In a skillet, melt the butter over medium-high heat.

Add the chanterelles and sauté for 10 minutes, then transfer to a bowl.

2 Cut the cheese into small dice. Wash and trim the chile, remove the seeds if desired (the more seeds, the spicier it is) and mince. Peel the onion and garlic. Halve the onion and cut it into thin slices. Mince the garlic. Put the cheese, chile, onion, and garlic in the bowl with the chanterelles and toss.

3 Toast the pine nuts in a dry nonstick skillet over medium heat until golden brown (stir occasionally). In a small bowl, mix the oil, balsamic vinegar, lemon juice, and basil. Pour the mixture into the bowl. Add the pine nuts, stir everything well, and let stand for 30 minutes to blend the flavors.

4 Wash the lettuce and pat dry. Split open the rolls, then toast them until golden brown. Line the bottoms of the rolls with lettuce leaves, and top with the marinated chanterelle salad.

Green Egg Sandwich

● easy
● sophisticated

Serves 2:

8 oz asparagus (ideally thin stalks)
3 tbs olive oil
Salt to taste
4 eggs
1/2 baguette (about 8 oz)
1/2 bunch fresh chives
Pepper to taste

Prep time: 20 minutes
Per portion: 600 calories
20 g protein / 32 g fat / 54 g carbohydrates

1 Wash the asparagus, then cut off about 1 inch from the lower, woody end. If the asparagus stalks are thick, peel the lower third with a vegetable peeler (peeling is not necessary for thin stalks). Cut the asparagus into 1-inch pieces.

2 In a skillet with a lid, heat the olive oil over medium-low heat. Add the asparagus and salt, and cook for 10 minutes, until tender-crisp. After 2 minutes of cooking, put the lid on the skillet.

3 Meanwhile, break the eggs into a bowl, beat gently, and season with salt. Cut the baguette in half crosswise, split open the halves, and toast them until golden brown.

Wash, shake dry, and mince the chives.

4 Pour the eggs into the pan on top of the asparagus. Cook, stirring with a wooden spatula, until the eggs are scrambled and cooked to your preference.

5 Distribute the scrambled eggs on the baguette pieces, sprinkle with the chives, and season with pepper. Serve the sandwiches warm, open-faced.

Variation

Substitute 2 1/2 oz fresh spinach, or 4 oz snow peas, for the asparagus. Before adding the eggs, sort and wash the spinach, and steam it in a skillet for 3-4 minutes. Or, wash and trim the snow peas, and steam them for 5-6 minutes.

Sandwich Provençal

● filling
◐ eat now

Serves 3:
1 small eggplant
Salt
1 red bell pepper
6 oz large brown
  mushrooms
1/2 red onion
1 medium zucchini
1 sprig fresh thyme
1/4 cup olive oil
6 slices whole-grain
  sandwich bread
3 tbs Aïoli (p 21)

Prep time: 50 minutes
Per portion: 520 calories
11 g protein / 33 g fat / 51 g
carbohydrates

1 Wash and trim the eggplant, and cut it lengthwise into 1/4-inch-thick slices. Sprinkle both sides of the slices with salt, and let stand for 20 minutes. Pat the eggplant dry with paper towels.

2 Meanwhile, preheat the grill or broiler. Trim and wash the red pepper and cut it lengthwise into eighths. Grill or broil the pepper pieces for about 8 minutes (if broiling, place the peppers on a foil-lined pan skin-side up), until the skin blackens and blisters. Let the peppers cool under a kitchen towel.

3 Trim, wipe clean, and slice the mushrooms. Peel the onion and cut it into fine slices. Wash and trim the zucchini, then cut it into sticks about 4 inches long. Remove the skin from the red pepper (see p 24, step 5). Wash and shake dry the thyme.

4 In a large skillet, heat 2 tbs of the olive oil over medium-high heat. Add the zucchini, mushrooms, and onions, and sauté until light brown. Add the red pepper pieces and sauté for 3 minutes.

5 Brush both sides of the eggplant slices with the remaining olive oil. Grill or broil the eggplant for about 3 minutes per side, until golden brown.

6 Toast the bread until golden brown, and spread with the aïoli. Layer the vegetables on 3 of the bread slices. Pluck off the thyme leaves and sprinkle them over the vegetables. Cover with the remaining bread slices, cut the sandwiches in half diagonally, and serve.

Sun-Dried Tomato-Avocado Sandwich

● fast
◐ eat now

Serves 2:
1 small, ripe avocado
1 small clove garlic
2 tbs sour cream
1 tbs lemon juice
Salt & pepper to taste
10–15 leaves arugula
5–6 oil-packed sun-dried
  tomatoes
1 ciabatta roll (about 3
  1/2 oz) or other crusty
  white bread

Prep time: 15 minutes
Per portion: 630 calories
10 g protein / 17 g fat / 47 g
carbohydrates

1 Cut the avocado in half lengthwise, remove the pit, peel the flesh, and mash it in a bowl with a fork. Peel and mince the garlic. Add the garlic, sour cream, and lemon juice to the bowl, and mix well. Season with salt and pepper.

2 Wash the arugula, pat dry, and remove the large arugula stems.

3 Cut the sun-dried tomatoes into fine strips, reserving the oil.

4 Split open the roll. Drizzle the roll halves evenly with the sun-dried tomato oil.

5 Divide the arugula leaves among the roll halves, then spread with the avocado mixture. Arrange the tomato strips on top of the avocado. Serve the sandwiches open-faced.

above: Sandwich Provençal
below: Sun-Dried Tomato-Avocado Sandwich

The Hamburger

This favorite of chain restaurants and backyard barbecues also belongs among the sandwiches. Though it gets its name from Hamburg, Germany, where it is thought to have originated, hamburgers have become ubiquitous on American restaurant menus and stand as a symbol of American culture. Making burgers at home is very easy, and they lend themselves well to many different variations.

A Burger Party

With hamburgers as the focal point, super parties can be organized, especially in summer, when you can grill outdoors. The patties, made from one or several kinds of ground meat or poultry, can be prepared ahead of time, covered and refrigerated until party time. The other garnishes can also be prepared ahead of time, leaving time for the host to enjoy his or her guests.

Some burgers, such as the Italian Burger (p 48) and Blue Burger (p 50) crumble easily, because the meat patty is filled with a nugget of cheese. These burgers are best placed on an aluminum pan on the grill; or, you can serve the cheese separately. The Fish Burger and Tofu Burger (p 52) are delicate and also break easily, and should also be grilled on an aluminum pan.

You can make any burger a cheeseburger. To do this, place a slice of cheese on the burger patty shortly before the end of the cooking time and grill it

Burgers & Buddies

for an additional 1-2 minutes, until the cheese begins to melt.

French fries, potato chips (homemade or store-bought), and coleslaw are perfect additions to the hamburger party buffet. Don't forget to provide plates and napkins, since hamburgers tend to drip.

Good beverages for a burger bash include beer, light-bodied red wine, sangria, or margaritas. Good nonalcoholic choices include lemonade, soda, and fruit-infused sparkling mineral water.

Mini-hamburgers make cool party snacks. The patty mixture that makes 2 regular-sized hamburgers makes about 10 mini burgers. Of the other ingredients, you'll need about twice the amount given in the recipe. Miniature buns are already available in many supermarkets and bakeries.

Accompaniments

A great sandwich or thick, delicious hamburger does not necessarily need a side dish. But a little something extra to nibble on the side adds interest to the sandwich plate, especially when trying to impress guests. Try a handful of crunchy, homemade potato chips, some spicy onion rings, or some piquant coleslaw next to the sandwich.

Putting it Together

Following are some ideas for pairing sandwiches with appropriate side dishes.
• Coleslaw (p 13) goes nicely with meat sandwiches.
• Veggie Slaw (p 55) is a good companion to poultry and egg sandwiches, with Turkey Burgers, Fish Burgers, and Tofu Burgers, and also with seafood and steak sandwiches.

• Potato chips, whether homemade or purchased, go well with everything. Or, try the Onion Rings (p 54) or even Spiced Popcorn (p 55) for a nice change of pace.
• French fries go well with almost all sandwiches—especially burgers. If you don't want to make them homemade, there are good frozen French fries on the market, which can be baked instead of fried.
• Steak fries—thick potato wedges with the skin left on—are particularly good with burgers and other hearty, hot sandwiches.
• Tortilla chips are a good alternative to potato chips. Serve them with a selection of salsas or dips.

• Raw vegetables, cut into small pieces, or mixed pickles and pickled vegetables can be served as a side dish with sandwiches and hamburgers. These are especially good choices for calorie counters.

Hamburger

● filling
● easy

THE classic

Serves 2:

8 oz ground beef
1 tbs sour cream
Salt & pepper to taste
1 onion
1 tomato
2–3 leaves green lettuce
2 cornichons (pickled gherkins)
2 tbs canola oil
2 sesame rolls
2 tbs mayonnaise
2 tsp mustard

Prep time: 20 minutes
Per portion: 660 calories
25 g protein / 47 g fat / 38 g
carbohydrates

1 Mix the ground beef and sour cream well, and season the mixture with salt and pepper.

2 Peel the onion and slice it into rings. Wash the tomato, remove the stem, and cut it into slices. Wash the lettuce and pat dry. Slice the cornichons lengthwise.

3 In a heavy skillet, heat the oil over medium-high heat. Add the onion rings and sauté for about 5 minutes, until golden brown; transfer the onions to a plate. Using your hands, form 2 equal-sized flat, round patties from the meat mixture. Add the remaining oil to the skillet, then the meat patties, and fry for 2–3 minutes on each side. The patties should still be slightly pink inside.

4 Split open the rolls, spread mayonnaise on one half, and spread mustard on the other half. On the bottom roll halves, layer the lettuce, patties, tomato, onion rings, and cornichons. Cover with the top bun halves, cut the burgers in half if desired, and serve.

Tip! Serve this with traditional accompaniments, like French fries, potato chips, or coleslaw.

Bacon Cheeseburger

● eat now
● a classic

Serves 2:

8 oz ground beef
1 tbs sour cream
Salt & pepper to taste
2 oz mushrooms (optional)
1 tomato
A few leaves crisp lettuce
6 slices bacon
2 sesame rolls
2 tbs mayonnaise
2 slices cheddar or
   medium-aged Gouda
   cheese (about 2 oz)
Oil for frying

Prep time:30 minutes
Per portion: 770 calories
35 g protein / 58 g fat / 29 g
carbohydrates

1 Mix the ground beef and sour cream well, and season the mixture with salt and pepper.

2 Trim and wipe clean the mushrooms (if using), and cut them into slices. Wash the tomato, remove the stem, and cut into slices. Wash the lettuce and pat dry.

3 In a skillet, fry the bacon over medium heat until crisp. Drain the bacon on paper towels. Add the mushrooms (if using) to the bacon fat and sauté for 5 minutes, then transfer to a plate.

4 Using your hands, form 2 equal-sized flat, round patties from the meat mixture. If necessary, add a little more oil to the skillet, then the meat patties, and fry for 2-3 minutes on each side. The patties should still be slightly pink inside.

5 Preheat the broiler. Split open the rolls and spread them with mayonnaise. Place the patties and cheese on the bottom bun halves, and place them briefly under the broiler until the cheese is melted.

6 Top the patties with the lettuce, tomato slices, bacon, and mushrooms. Cover with the top bun halves, cut in half if desired, and serve.

Tip! Don't like mayonnaise? Use ketchup or mustard instead.

Green Burger

● sophisticated
● filling

Serves 2:

1 green onion
1 small clove garlic
1/2 bunch fresh Italian
  parsley
6 oz ground beef
1 tbs sour cream
Salt & pepper to taste
2 tbs chopped pistachio
  nuts
4 oz fresh spinach
1 red bell pepper
1 tsp butter
2 tbs canola oil
2 French rolls
2 slices Romano cheese
  (about 2 oz)

Prep time: 35 minutes
Per portion: 630 calories
29 g protein / 43 g fat / 39 g
carbohydrates

1 Trim and wash the green onion. Peel the garlic. Wash and shake dry the parsley, and pick off the leaves. Finely chop the green onion, garlic, and parsley leaves.

2 Mix the beef, sour cream, parsley, onion, and garlic well, and season with salt and pepper. Using your hands, form 2 equal-sized flat, round patties from the meat mixture. Sprinkle with the chopped pistachios and press them gently into the meat. Wash the spinach, remove the stems, and drain well.

3 Preheat the grill or broiler. Trim and wash the red pepper and cut it lengthwise into eighths. Grill or broil the pepper pieces for about 8 minutes (if broiling, place the peppers on a foil-lined pan skin-side up), until the skin blackens and blisters. Let the peppers cool under a kitchen towel, then remove the skin (see page 24, step 5).

4 Melt the butter in a skillet over medium-high heat. Add the spinach and sauté for 3 minutes, until wilted, and season with salt and pepper. Transfer the spinach to a plate to cool.

5 In a heavy skillet, heat the oil over medium-high heat. Add the patties and fry for 2-3 minutes on each side. The patties should still be slightly pink inside.

6 Split open the rolls, and remove some of the bulk from the top halves. On the bottom roll halves, layer the spinach, cheese, patties, and red pepper strips. Cover with the top roll halves, cut in half if desired, and serve.

Italian Burger

● sophisticated
● eat now

Serves 2:

1 small onion
1/2 bunch fresh basil
2 oz mushrooms
6 oz ground beef
1 tbs sour cream
Salt & pepper to taste
2 oz mozzarella cheese, cut
  into pieces
3 tbs olive oil
10-15 leaves arugula
1 tomato
1 clove garlic
2 sesame rolls
10 black olives, pitted

Prep time: 30 minutes
Per portion: 640 calories
26 g protein / 48 g fat / 29 g
carbohydrates

1 Peel and finely chop the onion. Wash and shake dry the basil, then pick off the leaves. Trim and wipe clean the mushrooms, and cut into large pieces. In a food processor, finely chop the mushrooms and half of the basil leaves. Transfer the mixture to a bowl, add the ground beef, onion, and sour cream, and mix well. Season with salt and pepper.

2 Using your hands, form 2 equal-sized balls from the meat mixture. Push half of the mozzarella into the middle of each ball, then shape the balls into flat, round patties. In a heavy skillet, heat 2 tbs of the oil over medium-high heat. Add the patties and fry for 3-4 minutes on each side. The patties should still be slightly pink inside, and the cheese should be starting to melt.

3 Meanwhile, wash the arugula, pat dry, and remove any long stems. Wash the tomato, remove the stem, and cut into thin slices. Peel and finely slice the garlic.

4 Split open the rolls, and remove some of the bulk from the top halves, if desired. Drizzle all of the roll halves evenly with the remaining 1 tbs olive oil. On the bottom roll halves, layer the arugula, patties, and tomato slices, and season with salt and pepper. Top with the garlic, remaining basil leaves, and the olives. Cover with the top roll halves, cut in half if desired, and serve.

above: **Italian Burger**
below: **Green Burger**

Blue Burger

● eat now
● sophisticated

Serves 2:
6 oz ground beef
3 tbs sour cream
1 tbs green peppercorns
Salt to taste
2 ounces Gorgonzola or
other blue cheese
2 tbs canola oil
1 tbs chopped fresh Italian
parsley
Salt to taste
A few leaves of iceberg
lettuce
2 sesame rolls
1/2 avocado

Prep time: 25 minutes
Per portion: 600 calories
27 g protein / 45 g fat / 25 g
carbohydrates

1 Mix the beef, 1 tbs of the sour cream, and the peppercorns well, and season with salt. Using your hands, form 2 equal-sized balls from the meat mixture. Push half of the cheese into the middle of each ball, then shape the balls into flat, round patties.

2 In a heavy skillet, heat the oil over medium-high heat. Add the patties and fry for 3-4 minutes on each side. The patties should still be slightly pink inside, and the cheese should be starting to melt.

3 Mix the remaining 2 tbs sour cream with the parsley, and season with salt. Wash the lettuce and pat dry.

4 Split open the rolls. Spread the parsley-sour cream mixture evenly on all roll halves.

5 Peel the avocado, and slice it. On the bottom roll halves, layer the lettuce, patties, and avocado. Cover with the top roll halves, cut in half if desired, and serve.

Tip! This burger is really tricky to eat. It's best to serve it on a plate, and offer knives and forks for eating. Don't forget the napkins!

Curried Turkey Burger

● sophisticated
● prepare ahead

Serves 2:

1 small onion
1 tbs butter
1 tbs curry powder
8 oz ground turkey breast
2 tbs plain yogurt
Salt & pepper to taste
2 tbs sesame seeds
1 tbs toasted sesame oil
1 tbs canola oil
1/2 bunch watercress
1 cucumber
2 French rolls
2 tbs Mint Mayonnaise
  (p 21)

Prep time: 30 minutes
Per portion: 560 calories
30 g protein / 40 g fat / 23 g
carbohydrates

1 Peel and finely chop the onion. In a skillet, melt the butter over medium heat. Add the onion and sauté until transparent. Stir in the curry powder, sauté briefly, and set aside.

2 Mix the turkey, onion-curry mixture, and yogurt well, and season with salt and pepper. Using your hands, form 2 equal-sized flat, round patties from the turkey mixture, then coat them with the sesame seeds.

3 In a heavy skillet, heat the sesame and canola oils over medium-high heat. Add the patties and fry for 3-4 minutes on each side. The patties should have no trace of pink color inside.

4 Wash and shake dry the watercress. Peel the cucumber and slice it. Split open the rolls. Spread all of the roll halves with Mint Mayonnaise. On the lower roll halves, layer the watercress and cucumber, and season with salt and pepper. Top with the patties. Cover with the top roll halves, cut in half if desired, and serve.

Fish Burger

● fast
● sophisticated

Serves 2:

**8 oz mild white fish filets
(such as cod, snapper, or
sole)**
1 lime
2 tbs bread crumbs
1/4 cup sour cream
**2 tbs chopped fresh
cilantro**
1/4 tsp salt
2 tbs toasted sesame oil
**A few leaves of iceberg
lettuce**
2 soft French rolls
2 tsp mayonnaise
**1 1/2 oz trout caviar
(optional)**

Prep time: 15 minutes
Per portion: 480 calories
29 g protein / 29 g fat / 30 g
carbohydrates

1 Cut the fish into
pieces, removing any
remaining bones. Place
the fish in a food
processor, pulse until
finely chopped, then
transfer to a boil. Wash
the lime, pat dry, and
grate 1/2 tbs of the zest.

Squeeze the juice from
the lime.

2 Mix the chopped fish,
2 tbs of the lime juice,
the lime zest, bread
crumbs, 2 tbs of the sour
cream, the cilantro, and
salt, and mix well.

3 Using your hands,
form 2 equal-sized flat,
round patties from the
fish mixture. In a
nonstick skillet, heat the
sesame oil over medium
heat. Add the patties to
the skillet and fry for 3
minutes on each side,
until cooked through.

4 Meanwhile, wash the
lettuce and pat dry. Split
open the rolls. Spread
mayonnaise thinly on all
of the roll halves.

5 On the bottom roll
halves, layer the lettuce
and fish patties. Top each
patty with 1 tbs each of
the remaining 2 tbs sour
cream and the trout
caviar (if using), cover
with the top roll halves
and serve immediately.

Tofu Burger

● prepare ahead
● sophisticated

Tofu, made from
soybeans, is rich in highly
nutritious plant protein
and has many other
health-enhancing
properties. Tofu has a
very neutral taste, and
can be used with a great
variety of ingredients.

Serves 2:

6 oz firm tofu
**Walnut-sized piece of
fresh ginger**
1 egg white
1 tbs bread crumbs
1 tbs soy sauce
**1 tbs chopped fresh Italian
parsley**
Pinch of ground cumin
Salt & pepper to taste
1 tbs toasted sesame oil
1 tsp curry powder
**A few leaves of spinach or
lettuce**
1 ripe tomato
3 tbs alfalfa sprouts
2 sesame rolls
**2 tbs Mint Mayonnaise
(p 21)**

Prep time: 30 minutes
Per portion: 400 calories
14 g protein / 24 g fat / 32 g
carbohydrates

1 Mash the tofu with a
fork. Peel the ginger, and
grate it finely. Mix the
tofu with the ginger, egg
white, bread crumbs, soy
sauce, parsley, and cumin,

and season the mixture
with salt and pepper.

2 In a nonstick skillet,
heat the sesame oil over
medium heat. Add the
curry powder, and sauté
for 1 minute. Divide the
tofu mixture in half,
place each half in the
skillet, and shape into 2
large, flat patties.

3 Cover the pan and fry
the tofu patties for 4
minutes. Then, carefully
turn them over with a
spatula (they break
easily). Reduce the heat
to medium-low, cover,
and fry the patties for
another 6 minutes.

4 Meanwhile, wash the
spinach or lettuce, and
pat dry. Wash the
tomato, remove the stem,
and slice. Wash the
sprouts and drain well.

5 Split open the rolls,
and spread each half with
the Mint Mayonnaise. On
the bottom roll halves,
layer the spinach or
lettuce leaves, tofu
patties, and tomatoes,
and season with salt and
pepper. Top with the
sprouts. Cover with the
top roll halves, cut in half
if desired, and serve.

Variation
Top this burger with 2 oz of sheep's milk cheese, thinly sliced.

Tip! Serve the Fish Burger with small cherry tomatoes, accompanied by French fries or potato chips.

above: **Tofu Burger**
below: **Fish Burger**

Onion Rings

● a classic
◗ eat now

Serves 3–4:

3-4 onions
1 egg yolk
1/2 cup buttermilk
Dash of Tabasco sauce
1/2 cup flour
1/4 tsp salt, plus more to taste
1/2 tsp baking powder
Vegetable oil

Prep time: 90 minutes
Per portion (4): 280 calories
5 g protein / 20 g fat / 21 g
carbohydrates

1 Peel the onions and slice them thinly. Separate the onions into rings, then soak them in ice water for 1 hour.

2 Meanwhile, whisk together the egg yolk, buttermilk, and Tabasco. In another bowl, mix together the flour, salt, and baking powder, then pour it through a sieve into the egg mixture. Stir the batter well and let it stand for 1 hour.

3 In a deep fryer or high-sided heavy skillet, heat the oil to 375°F. Drain the onion rings and dry them well. Pour the onion rings all at once into the batter and stir them until well coated.

4 In 4–5 batches, remove the onion rings from the batter, letting the excess drip off and carefully place them in the oil. Deep-fry the onion rings for about 5 minutes, until golden brown. Using a skimmer or tongs, lift out the onion rings and drain on paper towels. Season with salt to taste and serve immediately.

Baked Chips

● a classic
◗ eat now

Serves 3–4:

3 large, firm, baking potatoes
2 tbs peanut or vegetable oil
Salt to taste
Chili powder or paprika to taste (optional)

Prep time: 45 minutes
Per portion (4): 110 calories
1 g protein / 7 g fat / 11 g
carbohydrates

1 Peel the potatoes, then rinse well.

2 Cut the potatoes into very thin slices (this works best with a mandoline or similar vegetable slicer) and soak in ice water for 3 minutes. Drain the potatoes and dry them well. Preheat the oven to 250°F.

3 In a large bowl, toss the potatoes with the oil until evenly coated. Line 2 baking sheets with aluminum foil. Arrange the potatoes on the baking sheets in a single layer, and season with salt. If desired, sprinkle the potatoes with chili powder or paprika.

4 Bake the potato chips for about 30 minutes, until crisp and golden brown.

Spiced Popcorn

● a classic
● prepare ahead

Serves 5-6

Walnut-sized piece fresh
  ginger
1 clove garlic
2 tbs butter
Pinch of pepper
1/2 tsp ground cumin
1/2 tsp curry powder
3 tbs vegetable oil
1/2 cup popcorn
Salt to taste

Prep time: 15 minutes
Per portion (6): 130 calories
1 g protein / 13 g fat / 5 g
carbohydrates

1 Peel the ginger and
grate it finely. Peel and
mince the garlic.

2 In a small saucepan,
melt the butter over
medium-low heat. Add

the ginger and garlic, and
cook for 1 minute. Stir in
the pepper, cumin, and
curry powder, remove the
pan from the heat, and
keep warm.

3 In a large saucepan
with a lid, heat the oil
over medium-high heat.
Add the popcorn, reduce
the heat slightly, and
cover the pan.

4 As soon as you hear
the first corn kernels pop,
take the pan off the
stove, and quickly stir in
the spiced butter. Return
the covered pan to the
stove and cook, shaking
the pan occasionally,
until the popping slows
to almost nothing.

5 Pour the popcorn into
a large bowl, and season
with salt.

Veggie Slaw

● prepare ahead
● sophisticated

Serves 4:

2 oz snow peas
1 piece leek (about 2 oz)
1 tsp butter
1/2 head green cabbage
  (about 7 oz)
1 tbs mayonnaise
2 tbs sour cream
1 tsp curry powder
1 small clove garlic
2 tbs peanuts, roasted and
  salted
Salt to taste

Prep time: 1 hour, 20 min
Per portion: 100 calories
2 g protein / 8 g fat / 6 g
carbohydrates

1 Trim and wash the
snow peas, and cut them
lengthwise once or twice.
Trim the leek, slice it
open lengthwise, wash
well (be sure to get

between the layers), and
cut it into very thin half-
rings. In a skillet, melt the
butter over medium heat.
Add the snow peas and
leek, sauté for 2 minutes,
then cool.

2 Wash the cabbage,
remove the core, and cut
it into very thin strips.

3 In a large bowl, stir
together the mayonnaise,
sour cream, and curry
powder. Peel and mince
the garlic, and stir it into
the mayonnaise mixture.
Add the sautéed
vegetables and peanuts,
and toss well. Season the
salad with salt, cover, and
let it stand for 1 hour to
blend the flavors.

Don't feel like baking a cake? Would you like to try something new? Tea sandwiches, both sweet and savory, are scrumptious and easy choices.

Tea Sandwiches

In England, tea sandwiches are traditionally served with 4 o'clock tea, but they taste equally good with coffee. Tea sandwiches are small, soft sandwiches filled with a variety of delicate fillings, and are meant to be served as a snack, rather than a meal.

Traditionally, soft sandwich bread is used for tea sandwiches; if you prefer a different kind of bread, be sure that its texture is airy and light. To make them look pretty, the sandwiches are usually presented without crusts, cut into little triangles, squares, or rectangles. Some devotees use cookie cutters to make whimsical shapes.

Sweet Sandwiches

Sweet sandwiches are appropriate for breakfast or for dessert, as well as for snacks. Children love sweet sandwiches, but they are also favorites of adults. Of course, kids are wild about peanut butter & jelly sandwiches. For this you can use the traditional crunchy or smooth peanut butter and your favorite jam. Or, experiment with different types of nut butters and fruit jams or curds for your own personal take on the PB& J.

Sweet & Small

Sandwich Party for Kids

Sandwiches are a favorite meal for children—not only because they taste good, but they can be eaten with their hands. A sandwich party for kids has the advantage that the host can make the food ahead of time, and the kids have a variety of selections to choose from.

Sweet sandwiches are universally appealing, but savory selections are also appropriate choices at a kids' celebration. Some examples are:
• Club Sandwich
• Bacon, Lettuce, & Tomato Sandwich
• Bacon & Egg Sandwich
• Classic Tuna Fish Sandwich
• Falafel Sandwich (reduce the amount of garlic in the sesame sauce)
• Hamburger

More Party Ideas

• Heat up mini-hot dogs and put them into mini rolls with cream cheese or the kids' favorite condiments

• For small children, make the sandwiches a little smaller than described in the recipes. If you use sandwich bread, cut the sandwiches into 4 rather than 2 pieces, or use cookie cutters to cut out funny shapes
• For older children, use colorful cocktail toothpicks or flags, with which the kids can skewer the sandwiches. These are available in supermarkets or party supply stores.
• Put out a tray of mini hamburgers (page 45) with the kids favorite condiments on the side.

Picnic Sandwiches

Ideal picnic sandwiches require no plates or silverware and can sit for a while in the picnic basket without becoming too soggy. Be wary of keeping the sandwiches at the right temperature. For example, if you choose sandwiches that use mayonnaise, cream cheese, or other dairy products, be sure they are kept very cool at all times to avoid spoilage. Good picnic

sandwiches include: Italian Panini, Marinated Chicken Sandwich, Pan Bagnat, and Garlicky Eggplant Sandwich.

Another picnicking idea is to pack the bread and other ingredients separately, and assemble them at the picnic site. This technique works well with the Smoked Chicken Sandwich, Ham & Brie Sandwich, Tuna, Caper & Olive Sandwich, Smoked Whitefish Sandwich, Greek Salad Sandwich, and Chanterelle Sandwich.

French Toast Sandwich

- eat now
- easy

Serves 3:
2 eggs
1/2 cup milk
Pinch of cinnamon
Dash of salt
1/2 pint fresh strawberries
4 oz cream cheese
6 slices stale egg bread,
  about 1/2-inch thick
2 tbs butter
Confectioners' sugar to
  taste

Prep time: 25 minutes
Per portion: 440 calories
13 g protein / 26 g fat / 39 g
carbohydrates

1 In a shallow bowl, whisk together the eggs, milk, cinnamon, and salt.

2 Trim and wash the strawberries, remove the hulls, and slice them.

3 Spread the cream cheese evenly on the bread slices. Top 3 of the bread slices with the strawberries, then cover the berries with the remaining bread slices.

4 Press the sandwiches together lightly. Place the sandwiches in the egg mixture, and let them soak up the mixture for 1-2 minutes on each side.

5 In a skillet, melt the butter over medium heat. Fry the sandwiches in the butter until golden brown on both sides. Sprinkle the sandwiches generously with confectioners' sugar, and serve warm.

Variation
Instead of strawberries, try filling the sandwiches with fresh dates, chopped walnuts, blueberries, raspberries or apricots.

Raspberry Delights

● fast
● sophisticated

Serves 2-4:

1/2 pint fresh raspberries
1/2 cup heavy cream
1/2 tsp sugar
Dash of vanilla extract
3 sweet rolls
3-4 tbs cream cheese
3-4 tsp raspberry jam
1 tbs nut brittle, such as
   hazelnut or almond,
   broken into tiny pieces

Prep time: 10 minutes
Per portion: 350 calories
6 g protein / 16 g fat / 47 g
carbohydrates

1 Sort through the raspberries. In a bowl, whip the cream until stiff with the sugar and vanilla extract..

2 Split open the rolls and spread all halves with the cream cheese.

3 Spread a layer of raspberry jam over the cream cheese, then a layer of the whipped cream. Top with the raspberries, sprinkle with the nut brittle, and serve open-faced.

Banana Nut Sandwich

● fast
● easy

Serves 2:

4 slices whole-grain
   sandwich bread
2 tbs cream cheese
2 tbs crunchy peanut
   butter
1 banana
Ground cinnamon to taste

Prep time: 10 minutes
Per portion: 530 calories
9 g protein / 15 g fat / 28 g
carbohydrates

1 Toast the bread until golden brown and cool. Spread 2 of the slices with the cream cheese, and 2 of the slices with the peanut butter.

2 Peel and slice the banana. Divide the banana slices among the peanut-butter spread slices, then sprinkle with the cinnamon.

3 Cover with the cream-cheese slices, and press together gently. Cut the sandwiches in half diagonally and serve.

above: Raspberry Delights
below: Banana Nut
Sandwich

Cherry-Walnut Tea Sandwich

● sophisticated
● fast

Serves 4:

6 oz fresh sweet cherries
10 walnut halves
2 oz cream cheese
4 slices whole-grain
sandwich bread

Prep time: 15 minutes
Per portion: 230 calories
8 g protein / 12 g fat / 26 g
carbohydrates

1 Wash the cherries, remove the pits, and chop the cherries into large pieces. Chop the walnuts, and toast them in a dry nonstick pan for 5 minutes, taking care not to let them get too brown (they'll get bitter).

2 Spread the cream cheese on the bread slices. Divide the cherries and walnuts among 2 of the bread slices. Cover with the remaining bread slices, and press the sandwiches together lightly.

3 Carefully cut off the crusts on all sides. Cut the tea sandwiches into small triangles or squares, and serve.

Watercress Tea Sandwich

● prepare ahead
● fast

Serves 2:

4 oz ricotta cheese (or
cottage cheese)
1 tbs plain yogurt
1 bunch watercress
4 slices sandwich bread

Prep time: 10 minutes
Per portion: 110 calories
6 g protein / 4 g fat / 14 g
carbohydrates

1 Stir together the ricotta cheese and yogurt until smooth.

2 Pick over the watercress, wash well, and pat dry. Set aside a few watercress sprigs for garnish. From the remaining watercress, pick off a generous handful of the leaves, chop the leaves, and stir them into the ricotta-yogurt mixture.

3 Spread the cheese mixture on 2 of the bread slices, and cover with the remaining bread slices. Carefully cut off the crusts on all sides.

4 Cut the sandwiches twice diagonally, to form triangles. Garnish the triangles with the reserved watercress.

Tip! If there is any leftover watercress, you can store it in a plastic bag in the refrigerator, and use it in a salad the next day.

Iced Choco-Mint Sandwich

● prepare ahead
● fast

Serves 4:

4 slices sandwich bread
10–15 leaves fresh mint
2 tbs crème fraîche
2 tbs chocolate spread,
such as Nutella

Prep time: 10 minutes
Cooling time: 1 hour
Per portion: 120 calories
2 g protein / 4 g fat / 16 g
carbohydrates

1 Toast the bread until golden brown, and cool completely. Meanwhile, wash the mint, shake dry, and coarsely chop the leaves.

2 Spread 2 of the bread slices with the crème fraîche, and spread the remaining bread slices with the chocolate spread. Top the chocolate-spread bread with the mint leaves, and cover with the crème fraîche-spread bread.

3 Carefully cut off the crusts on all sides. Cut the sandwiches twice diagonally, to form triangles. Wrap the triangles in foil and place in the freezer for 1 hour before serving.

Cucumber-Mint Tea Sandwich

● fast
● sophisticated

Serves 4:

2 oz cream cheese,
softened
1 tsp grated lemon zest
10–15 leaves fresh mint
2 oz cucumber
4 slices sandwich bread

Prep time: 10 minutes
Per portion: 120 calories
4 g protein / 6 g fat / 14 g
carbohydrates

1 Mix the cream cheese with the lemon zest. Wash the mint, shake dry, and chop. Peel the cucumber and cut into thin slices.

2 Spread the bread slices evenly with the cream cheese mixture. On 2 slices of the bread, layer the cucumber slices and mint. Cover with the remaining bread slices.

3 Carefully cut off the crusts on all sides. Cut the tea sandwiches into small squares or triangles, and serve.

> **Tip!** Most tea sandwiches are made with untoasted bread. If you prefer to use toasted bread, be sure to cool it completely before proceeding with the recipe.

Credits

Published originally under the title Sandwiches, ©1997 Gräfe und Unzer Verlag GmbH München.
English translation for the U.S. edition ©2000, Silverback Books, Inc.

Editor: Jennifer Newens, CCP
Reader: Vené Franco
Translator: Gerda Dinwiddie
Design and Production: Shanti Nelson
Design: Heinz Kraxenberger
Production: Helmut Giersberg
Photos: Fotostudio Schmitz; Fofostudio Eising (page 28); Fotostudio Teubner (pages 36, 61)
Food Stylist: Rudolf Vornehm

ISBN: 1-930603-50-9
Printed in Hong Kong
through Global Interprint,
Santa Rosa, California.

Xenia Burgtorf
Burgtorf was born in the USA, grew up in Germany, and is an enthusiastic transatlantic commuter. She studied graphic design in Munich, and today works as a photo stylist and still-life photographer in Cologne. She is the author of several cookbooks.

Reiner Schmitz
Schmitz began his professional career in Düsseldorf and Munich, Germany as an assistant for several food and still-life photographers. In 1989 he became an independent photo designer. Among his clients are business, advertising agencies, and publishers.